The Poems of Sascha Wagner

TENNESSEE VALLEY
Publishing®

2008

Library of Congress Control Number: 2008910270

ISBN-13: 978-1-932604-58-0

Published by:
Tennessee Valley Publishing
PO Box 52527
Knoxville, Tennessee 37950-2527
info@tvp1.com

Printed and bound in the United States of America.

Additional information about The Compassionate Friends can be found on page 203.

Acknowledgments

Many thanks to Sue and Karl Snepp for their dedication and tireless efforts on behalf of this project; to Sascha's close friend, Donnafred Hinman, for sharing her personal photos and recollections; and to the Estate of Alexandra Sascha Wagner for the copyright assignment that made this publication possible.

We have attempted to remain faithful to Sascha's unique style: her word combinations, her punctuation, the arrangement of her words on the page and the whimsical floral sketches that she scattered among her poems. These are all part of the charm of her poetry.

If Sascha dedicated a poem in its original publication, we have retained that dedication as it originally appeared.

Joyce Andrews, Editor

Sascha Wagner

Sascha Wagner

Alexandra Sascha Wagner's poems have been a source of hope and comfort to bereaved parents for many years. The widely popular books of her writings, *The Sorrow and The Light* (1992), *Wintersun* (1996), and *For You From Sascha* (1999) were preceded by three small booklets published by the Central Iowa Chapter of The Compassionate Friends: *With Love from Sascha* (1984), *Again from Sascha* (1986), and *The Heart Remembers Always* (1988). She was generous in allowing nonprofit organizations to reprint from her publications. It is safe to say that more writings by "Sascha"—that's how she typically signed her work—have appeared in TCF chapter newsletters than those by any other author.

Born in Bremen, Germany, Sascha emigrated to the United States in 1947. Her daughter, Eve, was born in November 1950, and her son, Nino, in October 1953. Nino drowned three-and-a-half years later; then on the eve of the 15th anniversary of Nino's death, Eve died of suicide. Eve and Nino were Sascha's only children.

Sascha earned degrees in literature and history from the Universities of Colorado (B.A., 1968) and Denver (M.A., 1975). Long involved professionally in various areas of the mental health field, she was introduced by chance to the Central Iowa Chapter of The Compassionate Friends in 1980 and, soon after, began a vocation that she was to pursue for the rest of her life: offering comfort and support to bereaved parents through her gifted writing, counseling and workshops.

As editor of the chapter's newsletter, and later through her more widely distributed books, Sascha reached hundreds, then thousands, of bereaved parents with words of understanding and encouragement that truly resonated with their lives. She spoke with special credibility to parents with no surviving children, publishing for many years the quarterly newsletter, *L.A.R.G.O.* (*Life After Repeated Grief: Options*). In 1998, Sascha was honored with The Compassionate Friends Professional Service Award in recognition of the widespread support and understanding her writing provided to grieving parents and their families.

Sascha lived in retirement in Denver, Colorado until her death in 2003. The executor of her estate awarded the copyrights to Sascha's writings to The Compassionate Friends, so that her eloquent verse might continue to motivate and encourage grieving families. It is with great admiration and appreciation for Sascha's life, her wisdom, and the legacy of her words, that The Compassionate Friends presents this comprehensive volume of her poetry.

Contents

At First

At First

At first
my very name was grief.
My eyes saw only grief,
my thoughts were grief.
And everything I touched
was turned to grief.

But now
I own the light of memories.
My eyes can see you,
and my thoughts can know you
for what you really are:
more than a young life lost,
more than a radiance
gone into night.

Today you have become
a gift beyond my grief,
a treasure to my world –
though you have left
my world and me behind.

Death is a lonely word.
Peace is a distant cry.
Hope bears the scar of grief.
Love is a life gone by.

Friend
is a knowing touch.
Peace
is a rising light.
Hope
     shines from memories
     and stands
     against the night.

Early Grief

I feel a lightless void inside
It has no name.
I know that others
say I am in grief.
But for me,
it is without a name,
a mortal distress
beyond words.

First Encounter

When grief first enters our life,
it tends to invade us –
completely and relentlessly.
We are without comfort, we do not feel pleasure,
we find no joy.
We ache in mind and body.
We feel weak and numb.
In the deepest core of our being,
we are ready to accept
that we will never know happiness again.
What's more, we feel that this state
is entirely appropriate, natural and irreversible.
Nothing can convince us that,
given time,
we can learn to live again.

But we will.

Time lets you heal.
Love lets you remember.
Give thanks
for love and time.

The heart knows many songs
and sings them well.
The heart knows images
and sees them, even
when life is much too dark
to light the eyes.
The heart knows many songs
we cannot hear.
        The heart is wise.

In the darkness
somewhere,
hides a song and a light –
close your eyes,
listen and wait.

A Life Lost

I have lost a life
– not my own.
But it would have been easier
to have lost my own life
than to have lost
the life I loved more than my own.

Desolation

I read many words.
I hear many sounds.
Why can I not comprehend
anything I hear, anything I read?

When you died,
did you take away with you
my senses and my mind?

I understand nothing.

Changes

Be aware that new grief
changes all of your emotions
for a time.

But grief does not change
all of your emotions
forever!

Some of your old feelings
will return to you.

Please be patient.

About Being Strong

Many people are convinced
that being strong and brave
means trying to think
and talk about "something else."

But we know
that being strong and brave
means thinking and talking
about your dead love,
until your grief begins to be bearable.

That is strength.
That is courage.
And only thus can
"being strong and brave"
help you to heal.

My name is grief
My name is hope
My name is love

The Only Child

Words are so small.
Words are too commonplace.
How do I speak
the meaning of that face?

Face of my child,
face of my child who died,
light of my world,
stay shining at my side.

grief cannot be conquered
like an enemy
grief can only be changed
from pain
to hope
from hope
to deeper life

Who Is To Say –

Love and death
are the most powerful
events in human experience.

Joy and grief
are the natural companions
of love and death.

Who is to say
that we could have
love and joy
if we had not
death and grief?

Confusion

Confusion of the mind –
always the question: Why?
Not even certain
what the question means.

What do I want to know?
Why do I want to know
when knowing changes nothing.

And more than ever
haunts me that savage
inquisition of despair:
Why do I live?
Why do I have to live?
Why do I have to live now?

Previously published in Eva Lager's book,
Knowing Why Changes Nothing.

Hold Me

I want to cry.
Just sometime, let me cry.
Do not demand
that constant smile from me.

I know you are
uneasy with my tears.
I need to cry.
Please, do not turn away.

I promise you
that I will smile again.
Tomorrow I
will be as light as air.

But hold me now
and let my sorrow be.
Just for today,
this moment: let me cry.

Husband

I saw the grief
behind your earnest eyes.
(You would give anything
to have your child again.)

I felt the helplessness
behind your silent anguish.
(You would give anything
to take this hurt away.)

> I know you learned
> to keep your tears in hiding.
> And you were taught
> few words to speak for solace,
> not yours, not mine.

I saw the grief
behind your earnest eyes.
And I will know
to understand and trust you,
loving father.

Incident Before Dawn

You walk through the house
looking for something...
Your keys?
Your glasses?
No, weren't you looking
for that old address book?

    You walk through the house,
    feeling like something lost...
    Are you looking for yourself?
        You walk through the house...
        Are you losing your mind?
        How can you tell?

You walk through the house
looking for something...
Are you trying not to remember
what you have lost?

    (You will find your glasses
        or your keys
        or your old address book
        or yourself and your mind
        in the morning.
                But...)

"Missing"

Today
I give my sorrow over
to those children
who are truly lost –
we know not where.

Today
I surrender my grieving
to those mothers
who do not dare
to look at yesterday.

Today
I give my sorrow over
to those children
who are now hidden
behind the cruel secrets
of a distant life
or sightless death,
we know not where.

Comparisons

It is useless to wonder
what grief is larger
or what grief is smaller.
The death of children
fills to ultimate endurance
every human dimension
for pain.
There is no need
to give rank to death.
We only have to recognize
that grief has filled
a whole life
to its ultimate boundaries.

Grief is the ceremony
of lost treasure.
Grief is the homage
you pay to the love
you were once blessed to share.
Grief is not an enemy.

Suicide

Once you were rich with life,
you were self-confident
and filled with beauty.

Until a darkness came
to seize your mind,
a force from out of silence,
an ache without a reason,
a pain without a name.

What was this darkness that
would not be conquered?
What force,
what reason,
what pain without a name
would use your hands
to take your life away?

Once you were rich with life,
you were self-confident
and filled with beauty.
Now we are left alone
without an answer.

Why?

After a while
you reduce
all of your tortures
to one simple question:
why!

You no longer say
"what if"
You no longer say
"how could it happen"
you only ask
why!

Until one day
you find yourself
sobbing the truth:
no one can ever know.

Wanting

Walking out of a long
and aching night...
wanting to be child and at home
    wanting to feel warm

Walking into a strange
and distant day...
wanting to weep and to sing
    wanting to feel safe

Walking along a dark
and haunted road...
wanting to find and be found
    wanting to feel peace

Process

I am standing aside,
seeing myself
with my own eyes,
but uninvolved.
I observe myself
in the process of losing myself.

Previously published in Eva Lager's book,
Knowing Why Changes Nothing.

What Will You Find?

In everyone
there is a secret place,
where the sorrow
        of a lifetime
tries to hide
from the painful touch
of recognition –
Good friend,
        if you share
        your secret place,
        what will you find?

Trust yourself!

You will recover

        your courage

in your own time,

at your own pace.

        Trust yourself!

Is not your grief
the affirmation
of your love?

Limbo

What is the use of living?
What is the use of my life?
I struggle for its healing,
but is it worth the struggle?

I have heard
so many proclamations
about life and its noble design.
But I am no longer convinced.
My life seems worthless.
Living itself seems worthless.

What am I healing
when I heal myself?

Previously published in Eva Lager's book,
Knowing Why Changes Nothing.

To the Dead Infants

They are gone
these young hearts
these flawless souls.
They are gone
and we must grieve
their loss –
we must remember.

But when we
begin to live again,
then we can be
each one of us
a heritage of humanness
a memorial of hope
a sign of closer understanding.
       In their name
       who are gone,
       these young hearts
       these flawless souls –
       in their name
       let our lives
              grow.

The Compassionate Friends in Brandon, Manitoba, Canada,
chose the last lines of this text for their Children's Memorial,
which Sascha had the honor to dedicate in May 1991.

Enigma?

Grief is a darkness
that answers no questions.
But love will give you
light on the path
of leaving your questions
behind.

How Many Days

How many days like these
must come and go
before my solitary grieving
finds an end?

And if my grieving
finds an end, some day –
Will I have
any feelings left at all?

One small life,
still casting its graceful light
into this world of large shadows.

One small life,
bright as a candle at dusking –
shared, in remembrance,
with sisters and brothers born still.

One small life,
giving to your heart and mine
a courage for finding the morning.

One small life –
Today and tomorrow, a promise
of tenderness deeper than grief,
of hopefulness stronger than death.

Still casting its graceful light
into this world of large shadows,
one small life.

Dedicated to Lindsay Nicole Gensler
and her sisters and brothers born too soon,
children of Dana and Phil Gensler.

Let sun and rain
and wind and flowers touch your heart,
yes, even touch
that hidden place inside,
where sorrow weeps.

Because the sun
            and rain
            and wind
            and flowers
are part of sorrow
with the touch of hope.

Ice Age

Yesterday you were with me
like a cool day in summer,
like a radiant song,
buoying my spirit.

Today you are gone,
and it is as if an ice age
has taken my life away.

Lonely/Lost

Loneliness is hard to explain.
Does it seem as if there is
no one to touch,
or is it an inner distance from you
to the next available person?
Loneliness is like
being a very small star:
millions of lightyears
from here to there.

Loneliness is a feeling
like being abandoned,
not having anyone to count on –
like a small child feels
when she is lost at the fair
– and it feels as if
all is lost forever.

Words

When grief is new
you need not find a reason
however good and brave
to temper your despair.

When grief is new
the heart accepts no answer
however wise and kind
to ease your mourning.

When grief is new
your life can only know
disintegration,
overwhelming pain...

>   My friend, try to believe
>   what other grievers learned:
>   you will not always hurt
>   as you hurt now;
>   time will restore
>   the soundness of your mind.

(All other words
are shadows on the wind
when grief is new.)

They Speak of Hope

Hope for a better future?
    What is a better future
    when you have had to lose
    that life so close to you?

    Hope for feeling better?
        What does feeling better mean
        when grief has mutilated
        all feeling?

Hope for hurting less?
    How can you hurt less
    when you are in an anguish
    beyond pain?

Only you have the answer.
    Find out what hope means
        for you.

Findings

Findings

The greatest comfort
at time of grieving
comes, quietly,
from the love that lives
within ourselves.

Dark Day

On a very dark day in winter;
when your eyes have forgotten
the color of apple trees...
on a very dark day in winter,
count the days – (sixty days?) –
        until spring.

On a very dark day in winter,
when your mind can't remember
the color of memories...
on a very dark day in winter,
reach for the healing kindness
        of time.

It Is True

"You will not always hurt like this."
These words are true.

If they do not reach
your heart today,
do not reject them:
keep them in your mind.

One morning –
not tomorrow perhaps,
but the day after tomorrow,
or the month after next month.

One morning the dawn will wake you
with the inconceivable surprise:
Your grief will have lost
one small moment of its force.

Be ready for the time
when you can feel for yourself
that these words are true:
"You will not always hurt like this."

The name of your dead child
is a magic word.
          Did you know?
At any given moment,
whether busy or still –
stop,
and think or say that name:

Something will happen.
And whatever that something is,
let it happen –
          even if it be tears.

The name of your child
is a magic word
to heal your heart.

Small Hand

The small hand
that held your hand –
how long ago –

The small hand
now holds your heart
against bitterness.

The small hand
that held your hand
can heal your life.

Look at yourself
in the mirror.
Say to yourself
"It is hard
to lose a child."
Say to yourself
"It is reasonable
to hurt."
Say to yourself
"Healing takes
time."
BE GOOD TO YOURSELF.

Lesson?

Grief shows you who you are
– more even than love,
or success, or adventure.
More than any other experience,
grief shows you who you are.

When a few moments of calm
begin to find you,
remember what grief has taught you
and who you are.

Solace

In the smallest hour of your day,
when you are alone
with things remembered,
questions unanswered,
and unfinished dreams,
        then:

            give to yourself
                    the gifts of your kindness,
            bring to yourself
                    the comfort of forgiveness,
            share with yourself
                    the mercy of your love.

Sobbing Out Loud

Do you wonder
if we should encourage each other to sob out loud?
Even sobbing out loud alone is better
than not sobbing at all.
            Some human cultures
            provide grievers with rituals
            for sobbing and screaming,
            like the women in some African villages,
            or the bereaved mothers of Islam,
            whom we should envy
            for the tradition
            of giving sound to their grief.
                    And what about grieving men?
                    Have we become so "civilized"
                    that we can only weep quietly?
                            Perhaps we should all learn
                            not to sob
                            in silence.

Now that your life
knows every darkness and sorrow,
now that your time
trembles with mourning and pain,
now that your eyes
see only empty horizons,
now that your hand
touches the center of grief:

Leave yourself open
to comfort and caring,
leave yourself open
to softness and friendship,
leave yourself open
to kindness and blessing.
    And try to listen
    for the still music of hope.

I am feeling fine today,
full of hope and warm and bright.
All my grief seems gone away,
and my memories are light.

Yes, I know this may not last.
But while laughter holds my hand,
I will let it lift the past,
I will let the gladness stand.

While this sunny moment brings
beauty for my heart to touch,
I will keep a thousand things,
rich and good and blessed things,
that I did forget...too much.

Strangers

Strangers walk the road with me
Strangers who are unaware
Strangers look at me and see
Only heaviness to share

And I turn my hurt aside
Waiting for one healing touch
But the strangers frown and chide
That I count my grief too much

Only now and then a friend
– someone who is grieving too –
Helps my broken life to mend,
And perhaps that friend is you?

Do we need to learn
that life is good
even when we hurt?

Do we need to say
that honesty and courage
do not insist
on banished tears?

Do we need to tell
the unsteady world around us
that life is true
when we invite it all –
not only cheer and fun
    but also pain.

This is a day when I can't laugh or cry.
This is a day when I keep asking "Why?"
This is a day when I regret and grieve.
This is a day when I will not believe
that love and joy and hope
were ever true.

And then, my friend,
I do remember <u>YOU</u>.
And then, my friend,
my life returns from stone.
And then, my friend,
I touch my heart and know:
this is a day we need not walk alone.

Friend,
       I may not know your name –
       nor have I seen your face.
       We have not spoken.

Friend,
       yet I know you well,
       because we share an heirloom,
       you and I,
       an heirloom cast by grief
       into the shape of love
       and care
       and understanding.

It has a name:
                COMPASSION

Sharing

When the most fearful solitude
            seems yours alone,
            when you are certain
            that there are no friends,
that no one feels as cast away as you –
when night and day and earth
            move on without you
and leave you, motionless, in icy pain –

when you feel mute with grief and isolation,
            when you seem cut
            from every living thing,
then listen to the truth
            your silence touches:

Behind oblique facades
            of noise and cheering
a thousand other lives
            are drowning, drowning,
in other sorrows and in other pain –
            afraid to cry for help,
afraid to break...

They need to hear your sorrow
            and your darkness.
Give them your truest self,
            discover theirs.
Reveal your tears –
            then share and speak your heart.

Did you make me cry again,

friend, who lets me be

      so many ways

(loud or sentimental)

patiently

     ?

Did you make me think again,

friend, who lets me see

      so many thoughts –

candles for the light of

memory

     ?

Did you make me smile again,

friend who knows that we

      are many things:

hurt and brave and somehow

rich and free.

Near Death

There are many ways
in which to have near-death experiences.
Being near-death can mean
being too close to death.
as you were
when your child died.

When grief
almost takes your own life away,
remind yourself that,
not long ago.
you were too close to death,
and now you need time
to heal from that encounter.

Say to yourself
"I will begin to heal
when my life recovers."
"I will begin to heal
when a smile can again
touch my heart."
"I will begin to heal
when I can."

Old Grief

It is a milder storm
and not so dark.
It lets you see the shore
where life goes on.

Old grief finds words of peace,
and brings us gifts
of memories and joys
from treasured living.

But nothing takes away
the emptiness
of all those years,
of all those haunted nights,
of all those lost embraces.

It is a milder storm,
but just as grave.
Old grief does hover
over soul and mind:
a heartbreak song
of timeless disappointment.

Traditions

Have you been taught
to cry without a sound
        (the tears descending
        like a cutting edge)
            ?

Have you been taught
to smile beyond endurance
        (your throat an aching
        lock around your heart)
            ?

Have you been taught
to owe the world your service
        until your mind seems
        not to be your own
            ?

Do not consent.
Truth teaches other lessons:
        grief needs to sob aloud;
        grief does not want to smile;
        grief wants to serve
        your inner healing, first.

Counselor

Find for yourself
the same kindness
as you would feel
for your very best friend.
     What would you say to her,
     if she were lost
     in guilty doubt.
     as you are now?
Would you not
counsel compassion
instead of finding fault?
Would you not
counsel tenderness
and soothing comfort
for her anguished spirit?

Listen to yourself.
You can be
your own best counselor.

Assignment

Find someone
 who is not
 in a hurry.
Find someone
 who needs
 to listen.
Find someone
 who craves
 to understand
 how you feel.

Be someone
 who is not
 in a hurry.
Be someone
 who needs
 to listen.
Be someone
 who craves
 to understand
 how grief feels.

Helping

Often, what needs to be done
are practical things,
like weeding the garden
or washing the kitchen walls.
Often what needs to be done
are quiet things
like listening to the same
painful story many times over.

Words are not always
the greatest comfort for grievers.
The things WE may want to do
are not always the best.
Try to consider what is truly needed.

Love is work.

Progress

On better days
I fill my life with laughter,
enjoy the charm
of other people's children,
and think about
new flowers for my garden.

On better days,
I start the morning proudly.
I disregard
the forecast of bad weather,
and look ahead
to possible adventures.

On better days,
I look at faded pictures,
recall vacations
in the rainy season,
remember kissing
baby-powdered feet.

On better days,
I hardly cry at all.

Small Signs

Since grief can make us lose
many of our own deep feelings,
we often disregard
what small signs of love we are given
by those who are in our life.

When grief makes us lonely,
it is difficult to appreciate
the small affections,
attentions, or connections
which come to us.

But those small signs
of loving attention
do deserve notice.
If we let them touch us,
they will give us warmth
and strength and hope.

Have you discovered the secret –?–
   often
   what makes you cry
   can also
   make you smile...

Pilgrim

Grief is like a pilgrimage
through arctic night.
You may be without daylight
for a long time,
and when the first sunrise
greets you,
the new day is brief.

But you will find
that the days grow longer
and more beautiful,
until one day the world
turns to gold again
and your life is aglow
with memories.

The Others

You may feel hurt,
because others do not seem to understand
what you need them to do for you.
Try to remind yourself
That, just like you,
those around you also feel lost
in your world of grieving.

It is not easy for you,
or for the others, to understand
what you need.
Therefore. you may want to say:
"I do not know
if I am able to ask for anything."
Or you may want to say:
"I do not know, what I need."
And you may ask them
to imagine what you might want
what you might need.

But when you can,
tell the others what you need.
This is important and essential
both to them and to you.

Teacher and Helper

This is a time
When you do not listen
To yourself.
This is the time
When you do not want
To recognize your needs.
Taking care of yourself
Is such a meaningless notion now.

Yet, these days,
More than any others,
Must have your help
In guarding your survival.

Life asks that you go on
        In your child's honor.
Because you will be a teacher.
Because you will be a helper.
Because you will be the keeper
        Of your child's memory.

Masks

At times of sorrow
everyone deals with feeling
in unique ways.

Try not to be hurt
if those closest to your heart
seem to grieve less
or behave strangely.

We cannot always see on the outside
how someone mourns on the inside.

Valse Triste

Spring again, spring again,
Lovely and warm and bright.
Spring again, spring again,
blossoms wait, smiling.

Spring again, spring again.
Memories look at me.
You will not see this spring.
You will not know this spring.
                Child of the other life,
                help me to dance.

Keep an open account of your life.

Do not discount your sorrows.

Do not discredit your joys.

Healing Takes Time

Did you wake up in the morning
with tears in your heart?
And did you say to yourself
"I should not feel like crying,
not like this, every morning"?

But you do know the truth, don't you?
When life deals us such a tragic blow,
such enormous damage,
we need many mornings to recover.
We need more than a few moments
                to heal.

Take for yourself the grace
of one quiet healing-step at a time.
Trying to rush the work of grief
will slow down your renewal.

You only need to remember
that you WILL recover some day.
You only need to remember
that we all have our own measure.
And we all heal at our own pace.

Journey

Life is a journey
between shadow and light
many times over

Travel your road
with readiness, always, for joy
and with loving attention
to the richness
        of your memories.

Uneasy Word

Hope is not an easy word for grievers
        but we, more than most others,
        need to understand
        what hope can mean for us.

Hope means finding the strength
        to live with grief.
Hope means nurturing with grace
        the joy of remembrance.
Hope means embracing
        with tenderness and pride
        our own life
        and the gifts left to us
        by those we have lost.

About Feeling Guilty

Do you blame yourself?
Are you strangled by the burden
of things you think you "should have done,"
as if these were the things
that killed him?

Dear Griever,
take time to realize
that death is not in your hands,
and blame is not the answer.

Try to relinquish
this relentless torment
Hold your heart now
with the tenderness
that human grief deserves.

Losses and Gains

In time of grieving,
you may encounter
      other unexpected losses...

Friends you counted on
may not be able
to stand with you,
may not be able
to give themselves to your need.

      But you will also find
      some unexpected gains:
      people you never counted on
      will be your friends
      and stand with you
      and give you strength.

They are the treasure
you will learn to cherish,
when you begin to heal.

Your hand touches me sometimes,
compassionate friend;
your eyes look at me sometimes,
smiling in tears.

You are with me so often,
compassionate friend:
a wordless answer
to unspoken questions.

You remind me always,
compassionate friend,
that love is not lost,
that I am after all not alone.

From a Friend

How much I want to say –
How much I want to be
the voice to comfort you
again,
the touch to make you free.

But all my words can mean
is to remind you here
that you will find the light
again,
the sun to melt your fear.

So take your time and cry.
My hands are holding you
until your heart may see
again
what spring and life and love
and hope can do.

Three Secrets

The secrets of healing from grief
are love (as in friend-ness),
patience (as in waiting gently),
and honesty (as in not covering up).

Try to learn finding these,
with love, patience, and honesty.

Friends

When our special sadness
comes to call,
when we remember
more than we can bear,
when courage falters –
shadows everywhere:
Then let us reach
and touch and share,
we, who are friends.

The Listener

I have told you the story,
more than a hundred times
So it seems.

And you have heard me again,
more than a hundred times –
So it seems.

One day, will I be able
to tell you how thankful
I am for your listening,
unfailing friend?

How thankful I am to you
for your quiet attention,
for your sweet understanding,
for your generous heart –

You have made me remember
the meaning of laughter and hope.
You have made me remember life
more than a hundred times
So it seems.

Anger

Grief often brings to us
a feeling of desperate anger.

But let us try to remember
that much of our anger is only
a reflection of helplessness
in the face of death.

Yet, that anger must be acknowledged –
anger denied
is an enemy of healing.

Relevant Question

Sooner or later you will ask yourself
whether your anger is greater
than your determination to survive.

Does your anger keep you
from loving those near and dear to your heart?
Do you think your anger should be
the same five years from now?

In many ways you may recognize
that love and peace of mind
are more important
than most mistakes.
Think about it?

Lifelink

Find in the dark of grief
the sunlit spaces.
Find in your sorrowed time
a moment's smile.
Find in the loneliness
of your despairing
one warm and kindred mind,
one hand to touch
your most secluded feeling.

– Find a friend.

Emissaries

My flowers lie with impersonal faces
on the ground where she rests.
My flowers do not speak,
they do not sing.
They only move
as the wind may touch them
or my hands.
But these flowers hide within them
the tenderness and the sorrow
of my grieving –
That is their secret, and mine.

Written for Eva Lager's Book,
Knowing Why Changes Nothing.

In the Morning

From wherever you are
        you smile at me.
"Find life for both of us"
        you say.
"Find peace for both of us"
        you say.
"Find strength and love and hope
        for both of us,
        because you are
                my mother."

Sunshine Thought

Deep in winter, my friend,
when life is darkest,
it is very important
to try thinking
one small sunshine thought
every morning, early.
Try your best...

Honesty

There is an honesty
to comfort us –
an honesty
that does not shrink
from sorrow –
an honesty
that lets us recognize
how life is more
than ignorance of pain.

There is an honesty
to give us hope –
an honesty
that sings the song of life
and keeps us singing
even while we grieve.

There is an honesty
to let us reach
for all of life's horizons,
as far as the heart can see.

Answers?

The memories are
bright and far away,
because
in all those grieving years
the pain has calmed.
The mind has learned
that life and loss are brothers,
that death tells nothing.
when we ask him "why."

The memories are
deep and long ago.
Here,
after all those grieving years,
the songs we sang,
the thoughts we shared,
the morning kisses,
and the mystic evenings,
remain alive in us
and unforgotten.

Now Love holds answers,
though we ask her nothing.

Anger-Work

Death can make us very angry.
We can be angry at life,
angry at God,
angry at the one who left us behind.

Anger is often only
a reflection of our helplessness
in the face of death.

Be aware that anger denied
is an enemy of healing.

A shift away from deeper sources of our anger
may seem easier to manage,
but such a shift will only increase
the strain and confusion
in a griever's overburdened life.
By trying to see our feelings clearly,
we can at least temper
the mental and emotional stress
which anger always carries.

Footnote from Sascha: It is important to remember again
that we should not be impatient if our anger needs time to
be resolved. Anger-work is part of grief-work. And grief-work
always takes longer than we think it should.

Facets

Grief casts a sharper edge on every day
and deepens all the shadows in your life.
>   For you, whose grief is not
>   one grief alone,
>   those shadows have
>   the sharpest edge of all,
> >   because the grief
> >   besieging you tonight
> >   restores again
> >   too many other sorrows
> >   and disappointments raging in your heart.

Grief asks so many questions, answers few –
grief takes away your patience
and your peace.
>   For you, whose grief means
>   losing everything,
>   those questions have
>   the sharpest edge of all.

There is but half an answer
weeping in the silence:
Find comfort and endure.
Remember love.

>   And wait.

Beware the critic
whose discomfort with life
lets him judge your grief
harshly.

The world stands waiting
to diminish the griever,
because the world is afraid
of grief.

Do what you can to heal,
but do not let the judges
punish your mind.

Give yourself permission to grieve –

do not deny any feelings that cry from within.

Grief, more than any other emotion,

lets you know who you are.

And some day "The truth shall set ye free?"

And some day you may even find

"The peace that passeth all understanding."

Someone else's child.
Someone else's name.
But the song is your song,
and the song is the same.

Hope is a tender song,
distant or near.
Music that waits for you
patiently waits till you
find it and hear.

when sorrow leaves your spoken words behind,
when only silence ponders in your mind,
when neither thought nor voice nor touching
                                    hand can find
an image or a language for your pain...
then do be brave and let your tears explain

Islands

Look for
the small,
quiet islands of peace
that arise
unexpectedly
from out of
the great sea
of your sorrow.

When a moment
of unbearable grief
strangles your heart,
close your eyes
and ask your dead child
what to do.

When your mind
cannot find an answer,
open your heart
and ask

for peace.

We all have
many secrets
in common.

Share one
and see...

Prescription for Healing:
Share a memory with
an understanding friend.

For Both of Us

As long as I can
I will look at this world
for both of us.

As long as I can
I will laugh with the birds,
I will sing with the flowers,
I will pray to the stars,
for both of us.

As long as I can
I will remember
how many things
on this earth
were your joy.

And I will live
as well as you
would want me to live
as long as I can.

That One Child

We travel through this life
in many climates
(the weather calm sometimes,
but often fierce).
We find the sunshine
and endure the shadows.
We falter often on the road, at night.

And many walk with us
who claim no sorrow,
and some who meet us
say they have not cried.
The world, they say,
prefers its play and laughter.
They say, we are
        uncomfortable company.

Let them be what they seem
and keep from envy.
Remember only this:
They never were
as close as you have been
to that one child.

Hope
is the child
of
sorrow and patience.

Watch the sunrise
Remember the laughter
Celebrate what was

Behind
each dark flower
of sorrow
waits
a memory
of the blessing
you shared.

Sascha dedicated this poem
to her dear friend,
Donnafred Hinman.

Bittersweet

Bittersweet

Bittersweet parents we are,

loving and giving still.

We render what tears

grief demands –

until, out of grieving darkness,

we come to celebrate

our children's life,

and our own.

Right now...
take a moment,
close your eyes
and remember
　　the smile of
　　your child!

Your name is solitude.
　　Because the child who died
　　was everything you had
　　in world and time.

You are alone today,
　　afraid to touch the wall
　　of questions keeping you
　　alone, alive.

One answer waits for you
　　(and what may follow?)
　　You are the imagelife
　　of your dead child.
　　You are his hope.

Your name is memory.

　　Dedicated to Judy E.

Treasures

Is this the first day
when you can bear to remember
how you smiled together,
that day in spring,
that morning in the rain?

Are you discovering
how many gifts of comfort
he left behind,
this child who died too soon?

His life is gone,
but he endows your time
from this day forward,
with all the faithful treasures
of remembrance.

Small things

    can be

    great comforts.

Remember

    the smallest things –

    they will make you smile.

Soon.

When your grief

is without memories,

let your heart find

the memories

that might have been.

Take strength

from your

memories

Give strength

to your

life ~

Message

When the child you have cherished is taken,
when the light of that promise is gone,
when the faith which sustained you is shaken
and your days stumble painfully on,

when the sorrows of loss are unending
and your God seems forever away,
find the message your lost-one keeps sending:
words of loving and thanking and mending...
let your child shape the peace of your day.

A Soldier from His Grave (with Love)

Dear Mother, O my Mother dear,
You cannot hear me now,
But I can see your secret tear
That you are 'shamed to show.

The world has told you to rejoice
Because I went to be
With other dead and risen boys
In Christ's eternity.

But God has told me yesterday
That you are right to weep...
For dying takes so far away
The son you could not keep.

Let warm
          memories

be as close
          to you

as the warmth
          of summer.

Remedy

Memories

will bring you love

from the past

courage in the present

hope for the future

In your gathering

of memories,

          invite your courage

          to remember

                    everything.

At a Concert (with Eve?)

Just by chance
the seat beside me
is an empty seat.
And my mind starts dreaming...

You are next to me,
and at the andante
you nudge me gently:
you look at me
with half a smile,
then you close your eyes
and pantomime a sigh –
we understand each other...

But the seat beside me
is an empty seat.

And when we have
remembered everything,
we grow afraid
of what we may forget.
A face, a voice, a smile?
A birthday? Anniversary?
No need to fear
                forgetting,
because
THE HEART REMEMBERS
                ALWAYS.

If the weather,

or the sky

or a place –

If a tree,

or the thought of spring,

or a mood

remind you...

Don't turn your heart away.

Let yourself remember!

Exercise (for Next Week?)

Try to teach yourself to remember
at the end of each day
that something nice
or important
or funny
or interesting
or beautiful
has happened to you...

Even though you may not be able
to enjoy such things just then,
keep your mind aware.

The Other Season

Look to the season of your memories –
it fills the weather of your life
        with mildness.
It turns to laughter what your
        mind remembers:
the sound of words, invented new
        for singing,
discovery of all-important secrets.

Look to the season of your memories –
it sets an ordinary past to music.
It changes ordinary tears to treasure.
It gives your faded pictures
        shape and color:
the touch of eyes, a walk
        in foggy twilight.

Look to the season of your memories –
how rich you were, and be how rich again.
Look to the season of your memories:
mourn and recall the child you love,
        you love…
until you lose yourself
        to find yourself.

Secret Eyes

Icy day in the morning.
— you walk without thought,
when, for a moment.
you see him again,
the child you took to school
on other mornings.

And from that moment
there comes to you
a string of images –
one following the other
in a misty flow of recollection.

Icy day in the morning,
making you smile,
making you weep,
making you wonder
how you can go on
without the child
who lives in the secret eyes
of your mind...
                    – but life carries you along
                       just the same.

Stars

The stars are like my memory of you:

They seem so small and frail up
       in the blue,
Yet they may each be greater than
       the sun.

And now, as faint as they appear
       to be,
the dimmest star, the smallest
       memory
is full of shining beauty,
       every one.

Can You Remember?

With winter tumbling snow
– the roses silent
and the water ice...

       with trees so barren
       that your mind refuses
       to picture leaves
       and green and even blossoms...

              can you remember,
              can you feel again,
              that spring did come
              from winter, every year?

Modest Triumph

Death has been in my house
too many times.
Death ran against my life
with poison lance.
Death took away tomorrow
in a shroud...

But death forgot to claim
my love for beauty,
ears for those summers past,
eyes for the fragrant snow
of bygone winters...

And death left to my mind
the recollections
of unspoken music...

Yes, death left to my mind
those many tears
those many smiles
to keep me whole.

Appears as "Gleanings" in
The Sorrow and the Light, published 1992.

Heartfrost

Does it not seem
as if in wintertime
your mind remembers
all those sunny things
that warmed you once?
And does it seem
as if you have not smiled
forever?

Now take your hands,
one in the other hand,
and do remember
all those sunny things again.
Again.
And let them warm you now.
– The smile will find you.

Remember

all things

very well –

     even many

     uncomfortable things.

All memories

make you richer!

Four A.M.

And does the bitter grief
keep you awake?
    Look at it full,
    as you would look
    into an avalanche
    sweeping your life away.

        Look at that bitter grief
        with conscious eyes,
        as you have looked on death.
        And tell your brooding sorrow:
        Yes, you know that death demands
        unwavering attention.

Do not avoid the truth
your mind repeats, repeats...

        And then there comes a truth
        beyond the truth –
        (no, do not turn away).
            Into your bitterness,
            love finds a way
            to give you solace.

And, yes, your heart will know
the sun when night has ended.

Midnight Gifts

The grief
that takes
your sleep away
at midnight,
it brings you hurt.
It also brings you love.

The Price

It is not really a question
of whether I could have wanted
never to have you with me,
if had I known
how deeply your dying
would break my life today.

There is only one certain truth:
Even if I had known
that there would come to me
the cruel grief I suffer today,
I would endure it all again
for the wonder of
having had you in my life.

Eulogy for a Murdered Son

Wise child, sweet son, great friend,
the world is colder
since your life was taken.
    Unbearable the absence of your touch,
    unspeakable the murder of your life –
    divorced from every solace is your death.

The only light left to these grieving days
is the awareness you were with us once –
so long ago, or was it yesterday?
    And now we own the gift of memory,
    how much you meant,
how rich and strong we were
    when we together
    shared our time on earth.

Unbearable the absence of your touch,
unspeakable the murder of your life,
divorced from every solace is your death.

    And yet.
    wise child, sweet son, great friend,
    the light you left behind
    will shine forever.

Oracle

Your child has died
        and only this is certain:
        that you will never be
        the same again –
        not what you were –
        not what you might have been.
Your child has died
        and grief may touch your vision
        with new and restless lights,
        with want and pain
        where once your life
        found reason, strength and peace.
Your child has died.
        The face of god is changing.
        It may be closer
        and more careful now
        or may seem cold
        and cruel, far away.
So trust your soul
        (however bright or somber
        however calm or fierce).
        Trust in your soul:
        – it will declare
                your answer and your hope.

            In time...

Letter on a rainy day in April.
Letter that does not need
            a postage stamp...
Dear Eve, dear Eve: I think of you
in mixed-up fragments,
I miss you with an unfamiliar feeling –
today is different from most other days.
            I don't know why.

How old would you be now?
Yes, thirty-four.
            (How young!)
And would you be like me?
You would be very bright,
I know for sure.
You would be melancholy –
is it the weather?
You would be much less sentimental
than I am.
            (Perhaps)

Dear Eve,
            we would be
            such good friends.

Dear Eve...

Leaving

Saying good-bye
    is not an easy departure.

Saying good-bye
    is not a breath and a smile.

Saying good-bye
    makes us feel frail and uncertain.

Saying good-bye
    takes one's composure away.

Saying good-bye
    even if only to travel,
    even if not for an "always"
    even if just changing place…

Saying good-bye
    means a mysterious future,

Saying good-bye
    conjures reminders of loss.

Thank you again
    for all the love and the sharing.

Tell me good-bye
    that I may travel in peace.

He was a spark of spirit and of heart.
He was the looking glass for nature's laughter.
He was a great adventurer on earth,
and now he journeys in the universe.

He was not flawless, but he was complete:
A human being in the finest sense.
He was the one I loved more dearly than he knew.
He was my own, my friend, my brother, David.

Dedicated to David James Gehrke.

Song

A song is on my mind –
a pleasant song, simple
and almost lighthearted.

Nothing else on my mind,
only the song,
singing itself over and over
all day long.

It is not a song about you,
but it is a song because of you.
And it means
that I miss you
all day long.

Vespers

Just at sunset
does your busy day
suddenly fall silent
and remember?

Does the rising night
make you ready
for seeing that face again,
feeling that touch?

Let the sunset
do its magic.
Invite the rising night
to cast its dream.

Have we not said
a thousand times and more
that we are richest
when the heart remembers?

To Our Surviving Children

and you were with us
    when the darkness came
    you stood and grieved
    and kept yourself alive

        We thank you now

we have not always
    honored who you are
and often did not tend
    your hidden sorrows

        Forgive us now

because you loved us
well enough to wait
until we could
return to you and know
with joy and hope and love:
        you are tomorrow

        We celebrate your life –

and while we well remember always, always
the one, the many souls who did not live,
    we see you once again
    for what you are:
    the wealth you are,
    the comfort
    and the promise

        We thank you now

To My Daughter Eve
born on November 4, 1950

How would it be if you were with me now?
What would we say, what would we do together?
I think we might be waiting for the frost,
and we would relish this Octoberweather.

And would we worry over waistlines spreading?
Oh, surely we would speak about some beau.
But we would soon leave smallish talk behind us
to wonder over things we do not know.

And we would fret about the same old questions,
why do we make mistakes (and more than once)?
Why doesn't love stay new and strong and tender?
And why do people fill the world with guns?

I think we might be waiting for the frost,
and we would relish this Octoberweather.

What would we say, what would we do together?
How would it be if you were with me now?

Nino
Born on October 28, 1953

Small son, you died
too many years ago.
You are so far away,
far in the past.

I have not spoken
to your photograph
how many years now?
I forgot to count...

I never dared imagine
(when you died)
the mindless water
burying your face.

But I remember still
the love between us.
And in remembering
I recognize:
your golden life
forever touches mine.

Sometimes
on a Sunday morning
(life around you
warm and silent)
Sometimes
in that golden hour
when your face
is yours alone:
feel the small hand
touching your hand,
see those earnest eyes
that meet your eyes...

Hear the sounds
of love remembered
on a Sunday morning,
sometimes.

Image

A breath of summertime
drifts from the rising sun,
comes from beyond the trees,
hums at your window –

A breath of summertime
smiles at your dusty face,
weaves into cloud and light
visions remembered –

A breath of summertime
touches your secret tears,
brushes the tears away –
(but not the image)

Legacy

Memories are a legacy
of hope and courage,
left to help us go on
when the giver is gone.

Remembering...

Spring is not far away –
there is a smell
of growing things about.
The snow looks somehow
even more perishable now.

Spring is not far away –
and memories move to another place.
Remembering: A squeaky swing
in the garden,
going back and forth,
back and forth...

Remembering: a bicycle taken out
for its first ride...
Remembering: incredibly wet boots,
cold hands, kissing-fresh face...

So many things remembered.
How many lost?
Not one, not one.
The heart remembers always.

Spring is not far away.

When the time comes
for lighting festive
                    candles,
let them remind you
not only
        of what you lost,
but also
        of what you had.

Also published as "Hanukkah,"
in *For You from Sascha.*

I thank you for that sharing in the morning,
when you reached out and let me know your sorrow
and let me see your life without disguises,
though I had only tears and said no answer.

And now, as summer moves, you still console me –
I feel your trust again, and I remember
how rich a gift: the closeness of that moment,
when grief and love met in a daughter's name.

Dedicated to Steven C.

Her name is Sonja, and her life was brief.
She leaves behind the memory of beauty.
She leaves behind a silence and a song.

She saw the world with tears beyond the smile.
She saw the world in gladness and in shadow.
Her name is Sonja, and her life goes on.

Her name is Sonja, and her music lingers.
Her image walks with us into the seasons.
And mornings gleam with memories of her,
And evenings hush in wistful recollection
of hours spent in soft togetherness.

Now she is gone from earth – a golden moment.
But even gone, she touches us again.
Because she once was here, she moves us still,
She moves us with the legacy she left us:
the gift of vision for a deeper life.

Her name is Sonja.

Dedicated to Sonja Epp, daughter of Ruth and Gerry.

At Dusk

Light a quiet candle.
Blow a quiet kiss.
Say a quiet fare-thee-well
to the one you miss.

Light a quiet candle.
Shed a quiet tear.
Sing a quiet lullaby
and the quiet Christmas Star
        will hear.

Candles

It is not easy to remember dead children.

But, easy or not,
we know that we will not –
and do not want to –
forget them.

Therefore we reach out together again,
to love them and to celebrate their memory.

Again, we light their special candles
and we say their beloved names.

We remember our children, who died.
They remain forever part of us,
and we are richer for having shared their lives,
however briefly.

Full Circle

Full Circle

The year has gone again
from spring to winter –
and in this year,
your memories may have found
a breath of calm between them,
quiet respite – sometimes.

Then why must there be
twice as many now –
these feelings, now,
these visions, songs and voices,
from Halloween to New Year's:
Twice memories and smiles
Twice memories and tears...

You know the answer,
even while you cry:
the tears are
(like the smiles)
the season's face of love.

January 5

It is children's day in Japan today –
For you, is it children's day
every day, and again, and always, now?

Let us send love to the children
wherever they are.
Wherever they are held
in a father's arms,
or in a mother's memory...
every day and again and always.

Winter Grief

Grieve as if to find eternal winter,
ache as if to banish every spring.
In your broken footstep follows mourning
for the children who were with you once.

Grieve as if to keep the day from dawning,
weep as if to kill each song you shared.
But be ready: when the sun grows stronger,
spring will yet reclaim your loving heart.

On a Very Foggy Morning

What a day today!
What a fog, what a misting –
Not being winter nor spring –
Not any season at all?

What a day today!
What a silence inside me –
Neither a warmth nor a grief –
Not any feeling at all?

What a day today!
What a stranger I must be,
now, to my very own life.
Not any person at all?

What a day today!
What a grayness awaiting
something –
                a song, or a touch,
or any season at all.

Windows

The breath of winter
painted fragile stars
on all the windows
of my quiet house.

And there I found
your face,
more fragile even
than the season's art,
a wonder to my eyes.

How can it be
that winter paints
such secret things
in white-and-silver sheen
for those who cry alone
at frosted windows?

Another Year...

Old year has gone away
with gift and candle –
old year has gone away
with thought and song.

Old year has given light
and dark and season.
Old year has been too short
and been too long.

Old year has given joy
and disappointment
Old year has given grief
and strength to cope.
Old year was memory
and was forgetting –
Another year is come:
give it your hope.

You Are Called

Into the rivers of eternity
The human mind adds, new,
a grain of time
and calls it by its weighty name:
One year.

Friend, you are called
to be a part of it,
part of this year –
and part, however small,
of universe and of eternity.

Warm Winter Day

How welcome,
right now, right here –
at the beginning of one more year –
                    is this day
with a kindness like summer.

Memories
shine in the sun:
right here, right now,
out of the gray
we call winter
    warms you
the thought of a child.

Also titled "Warm Day in January"
in *The Heart Remembers Always*,
published 1988.

Winter, Still

The sunshine lingers
on the muted earth,
as if to ask its inward world
            for flowers.
And what about
the stubborn rules of ice?
The sunshine lingers...

This day is gentler
than it ought to be,
as if to move my wintry heart
            to dancing.
And what about
the dark behind my eyes?
This day is gentler
than it ought to be...

First Anniversary

I know the world
is still the same
and life goes on.
The hours run
with ancient speed
from day to day.
I know.

And mornings are
the same new wonder still,
and music moves
the mind with secret hand.
And flowers grow,
and children sing.
I know.

But you are gone
and I am not the same
– am only half,
And half of me
            is gone away with you.

            I know.
            I know.

Wintersun

There are those days in winter
when your world is frozen
into a vision of eternal ice,
when earth and air
are strangers to each other,
when sound and color seem forever gone.
   There are those days in winter
   when you feel like dying,
   when life itself surrenders you to anguish,
   to total mourning and to endless grief.
And then it happens: from the bitter sky,
a timid sun strides to his silent battle
against the gray and hostile universe –
it changes ice to roses, sky to song.
   And then it happens that your heart recalls
   some distant joy, a gladness from the past.
   A slender light at first, then larger, braver,
   until your mind returns to hope and peace.
Let memories be beauty in your life,
like song and roses in the wintersun.

Dedicated to Randy Misita,
son of Bernie and Tony, brother of Angela.

"So generous a heart
So kind and forgiving"

February

Let this cool and
                gentle
month of the heart
remind you
not only of lost
                treasure,
but also of riches
(past and present)
                in your life.

Valentine's Day

Did you know?

When we truly listen

to each other,

we are saying

~~ I love you ~~

From **For You, from Sascha**, published in 1999.
A slightly different version appears in **Wintersun**,
published in 1996.

Before you know it,
here's another March
with daffodils and crocus –
any hyacinths?

Before you know it,
here's another sorrow –
the grieving over things
she used to sing about.

Before you know it,
here's another greening
with quiet hope
and modest promise –
listen, when you can.

In March

The year moves on.
Between the weeks and days
are spaces filled
with more than only time:
those minutes, moments,
when your life stands still
and aches in memory...

And part of you
needs to endure the dark,
because it means
to have that love again.
And part of you
prays for forgetfulness,
because your mind
may break, remembering.

Between the weeks and days
are spaces filled
with more than only time.

Spring, Soon

Is this our season
more than some other
turn of the year?
Is it?

With winter dancing
out and in,
freezing the melted snow
one more time?

Is this the season
between death and life.
Is it?

With sorrow struggling
in and out,
finding the touch of hope
one more time?

Spring Waiting

Winter's end is almost here.

Crocus struggle in the snow.

Sunlight has a softer glow.

     — Is the winter long this year?

Spring waits, watching for a cue...

not to rush your grief away,

but to be there, when you say.

     — Spring is waiting, friend, for you.

Find a little time for spring,
even if your days are troubled.
Let a little sunshine in –
let your memories be doubled.

Take a little time to see
all the things your child was seeing –
and your tears will help your heart
find a better time for being.

Counting...

Time to count the crocus on the lawn
(seven white, four yellow,
thirteen blue).
Windy sunshine breathing ice away,
and the trees are trying to be new.

You are not ready for spring, you say?

But spring is ready for you!

Passover

Counting the years,
Blessings and tears,
Counting the children
Who are gone
        From this earth.

Counting the memories
Of times past and done.
Blessing the children
On earth in this day of life.

April

(Time for jesting,
time for laughter?)

And if you are not ready,
not yet,
to remember something
that makes you laugh,

tell April to be patient.
Take your time.

Easter Thoughts

One more winter overcome,
one more darkness
turned to light and promise.

Winter is the price for spring.
Struggle is the price for life.

Even in sorrow, remember
to prepare your heart
for celebration –
next spring perhaps.
Or the spring after that...

The Children of April Nineteenth

Let these children
forever remind us
that our souls may be
in greater peril than theirs.
Let these children
forever remind us
that we are the ones
to need their blessings now.
Let these children
remind us to pray
that time has not run out
for us.

In memory of the children who died in Oklahoma City
and of all children in the world who fall victim to the
mindless cruelties of our time.

Mother's Day

How is the weather now,
on mother's day?
Shining with spring,
promising early roses?

But hides there, in secret,
a moment of grief?
Frost in the sunlight,
pale heartache of sorrow?

The children are gone.
Are you reminded twice over:
the children are gone?

And will you be ready perhaps
to remember without tears
the sunlight, the laughter, the roses,
you shared with the children
on next mother's day?

Just Spring?

This is no ordinary spring at all.
It dances on with unbecoming weather:
now more like winter than December was,
and then again as soft as early summer.

This is no ordinary spring at all.
It meets your heart with
                    unexpected dangers:
now with the loneliest of memories,
and then again with unforgotten laughter.

This is no ordinary spring at all.
This is like life itself, a changing season.
Accept the wintertime of grief, and then
reach for the hope of summer and of healing.

Spring/Time

The days are getting longer, longer,
and it is easier to work away.
So many things to do...keep busy, busy.
The more we do, the less we have to say.

The days are getting warmer, softer –
and is it easier to work a lot?
Alright, forgive yourself for crying midnights:
the heart remembers what your hands forgot!

May Morning

The morning colors
love and ache together
into the shape that life intends to be:
– As memories whelm secret territories,
      your mind takes note
      of sorrow, time and place.

The morning moves you
through familiar paces.
– While thought confirms another day in spring,
      your heart reminds you
      that your child is gone.

Lilacs

Come, look at May with me.
The world is music.
The lilacs laugh
and every meadow sings.

Your heart forgets to think
of spring or summer,
forgets the grief
that happened in the snow.

Until a memory
moves into sunlight
to bring the child,
the child who is not here.

Still, look at May with me
and hear the music.
And – for a moment –
hear the lilacs weep.

Thoughts for Springtime?

Would it be easier,
    if spring were not so lovely?

Would it be easier,
    if robins did not sing?

Would I be stronger,
    if the trees were barren
    or if a cloak of grey
        hid everything?

Could I be braver,
    if the days were faded
    and if the sun remained
        remote and cold?

I hear the whispers
of a new beginning.
    The earth is new.
    Why is my grief so old?

Memorial Day

For each grave
Where a soldier lies
At his rest

For each prayer
That is said today
Out of love

For each sigh
Of remembering
Someone who died

Let us also give thought to
The mothers and fathers
The brothers and sisters
The friends and the lovers
Whom death left behind.

School's Out

That time of year again,
when children move
from classroom to reality.

And deeper even than before
your heart recalls the child
who left this life
to move from here
to ultimate reality.

Give blessing to that journey,
when you can.

Father's Day

Warm and sunny day in June,
father's day.
Children, small and grown
give gifts to father
say thanks to father
say I love you.

But there are fathers
whose children are not here
to give gifts and say thanks
and say I love you.

Remember the fathers
whose children are gone,
because all too often
they grieve in heartbreak silence.

Summer Soon...

Sunlight dancing in the branches
of the birchtree at my door.
Meadow stretching smug and lazy,
darker, greener than before.

Wind as warm as hugging children,
clouds so round and very close –
and on one small grave there trembles
lovingly an early rose.

Summerwind

The one who owns this summer is not here,
not here to know the tender summerwind,
not here to share the glowing and the song.
The one who owns this summer did not live,
not live to touch the richness of this day,
this day in summer when you are alone.
Weep to the summerwind, weep and love again
the one you remember.

Vacation

I still remember
when I could not sleep
at three a.m.
Awake and dark,
I did not want forgetting,
night after night.
    Night after night.

I still remember
when I could not sleep
at three a.m.
Alone and mute
I sobbed the same old questions
into my mind.
    Out of my mind.

I still remember
when I could not sleep
at three a.m.
And yet, today,
I find us new with laughter
here in the sun.
    Here in the sun.

Summer's End

Always at summer's end
there comes that moment
when memory brings to me
gifts from the past.

I see your faces then,
glistening in the sun.
I hear your laughter then,
shared by the wind.

And in that glint of time
I feel you near again,
as you were, long ago,
at summer's end.

August

The summer runs to harvest –
Do you ask:
How can a harvest be without my child?

Friend, some day soon
the harvest in your life
will bring you hope and wealth
     from love remembered.

Another Summer

Leaving another summer behind,
adding one more bouquet
to your stores of remembrance,
holding new images
summerwarm to your mind.

Leaving another summer behind,
with old, familiar mementos
of long-ago times in the sun.
And did you discover once more
how grief changes memories
to anniversaries?

Sunrise

Can it be true:
        this is an easy morning?
The day escaping from
        its dark confinements,
while sun starts brushing
        earth with silken warmth.
No strain at all.
No hurry anywhere.

Can it be true:
your mind is whole and steady.
Now you remember things
        as once they were
on other mornings, then,
        and other days...

Can it be true:
this is an easy morning?
Remembering does not hurt?
        And you can close your eyes,
        and you can see,
        can smile – at sunrise.

        This is an easy morning.
            Use it well.

Now Autumn

What a strange time is autumn.
More than a season,
autumn can be like a mood.
Softness and warmth and abundance
drift from the sky like a smile.

And you remember the seasons
before the children died.

They do seem far away sometimes,
those seasons, now.
But not the children –
they are always here
in this strange time, this autumn,
when the softness
and the warmth
and the abundance
of unseen children
drift from the sky like a smile.

When autumn lingers in the gleaming trees
with painful beauty,
golden melancholy –
when we recall the wealth of bygone harvest
and wait the haunting of a lifeless winter –
hope is so far away,
spring is so far away.
But spring will come!

September: Monarchs

Time between summer and winter.
Time under changing skies –
muted and heavy with foresight,
or endless blue, smiling at butterflies.

Time between summer and winter.
Time between laughter and tear –
harvest of beauty remembered
and voices (where are you?) to hear.

Time between summer and winter,
thoughtful and painful and wise –
muted and heavy with losing
but smiling at butterflies.

Indian Summer

This may well be
the softest time of all.
Does mild September
still surprise your mind
with memories you thought
you would not have?

Believe me, friend, that
(after many tears)
this may well be
the softest time of all.

After October...

and if there be a perfect month,
for me, it is october –
with days and nights like laughing fauns,
with mornings bright and sober.

when wind will dance in sudden glee
to do the autumn-sweeping
or cloud and fog and wistful rain
can move a heart to weeping.

and in october You were born,
four days before november –
and four years later You were gone,
my little son, my only son,
I love you.
                    and remember...

Halloween

It is here, this day of merriment
and children's pleasure.
Gremlins and goblins
and ghosties at the door
of your house.

And the other children
come to the door of your mind.
Faces out of the past,
small ghosts with sweet, painted faces.
They do not shout.

Those children
who no longer march laughing
on cold Halloween night,
they stand at the door of your mind –
¬and you will let them in,
so that you can give them
the small gifts of your Halloween –
                        a smile and a tear.

November Again

November again, almost winter.
Muted world outside,
faded red, misty yellow –
fog in the morning.
Even the hardest wind
seems kind enough,
because we know,
we know that stormy blades
lie waiting.

November again, almost winter.
Gently the heart reaches
for the awareness of things to
                          come.

Holidays, so we call them.
Gently, the heart turns to
                        Christmas –

Songs everywhere. And lights.
Gently the heart must remember
the things gone by,
the time gone by,
the child gone by.

November again.

In Fall

Things often are
most beautiful
before they leave us –

As autumn ends,
she spends her final glory
on us, who hurt
when we remember spring.

How Soon – –

(How Soon Is Winter!)
Seasons racing by
with timeless haste –
    Spring just a fleeting moment
    – summer gone.

Then autumn holds the heart
with brief perfection.

How soon is winter.
And how much remembered
    underneath the snow
are songs, and flowers,
    harvest wealth
    and children.

Giving Thanks

I can not hold your hands today,
I can not see your smile.
I can not hear your voices now,
My children, who are gone.

But I recall your faces still,
The songs, the talks, the sighs.
And story times, and winterwalks,
And sharing secret things.

I know you helped my mind to live
Beyond your time with me.
You gave me clearer eyes to see –
You gave me finer ears to hear –
What living means, what dying means,
My children, who are gone.

So here it is Thanksgiving Day,
And you are not with me.
And while I weep a mother's tears,
I thank you for the gift you were,
And all the gifts you gave to me,
My children, who are gone.

Speaking Love

Thoughtful mornings in November,
winter gray and chill at twilight.
Soon there will be colored candles.
Soon there will be celebration.

Do not force your heart from sorrow
at this time of happy splendor:
this is also time for speaking
love to dead and silent children.

Solstice

The year has turned again.
As quickly as it came,
it runs away.

The year has turned. Again
before us waits
another string
of sparkling celebrations...

How fine and welcome
are the holidays.
How sharp and painful
are the holidays.

Dark with the light,
grief with the joy,
life tumbles on.

Hanukah

is our

Festival of Lights.

Let your light shine,

so that their light

may shine.

Wintersong

Season of lights, season of love and peace
Season of shadow, season of memories,
Season of warmth and joy, season of secret tears:

Give us the courage to laugh again
Give us the vision to hope again
Give us the power to love again –
                    For all our new seasons
                    And all our new years

Yule

The song of yuletide rings
with tears and laughter.
        And if you listen deeply,
        you will find
        the sound of every voice
        you ever knew.

time to open the Christmas door.

time to let the season cheer you.

time for singing a Christmas song.

time to wonder...can he hear you?

time to stand in the dark, alone —

darker and lonelier than before.

time for turning to share the light.

time to open the Christmas door.

The time of Christmas
                    rings
with tears
        and laughter.

And if you listen
                deeply,
you will find
the sound of
        every voice
you ever knew.

'Tis the Season

It is trying to be
A warm and loving time,
With kindness and light,
And a feeling of hopeful renewal.

Find what blessings you can.
Help your heart to remember
That the children who died
Are about us, everywhere,
Trying to make this,
Even for you,
A warm and loving time.

Thoughts at Christmas

There was that other child
        born in the stars –
He did not stay in life
        beyond his summer.

There was that other child
        who touched the aching world
with love and hope.

Now, for that child and yours
        (and when your heart inclines),
have time to touch the aching world
        with love and hope.

At Christmas

I reach for the laughter of Christmas,
around me are music and light.
The air arches clear into heaven,
a mirror of gold and of white.

I touch it, the laughter of Christmas.
The stars are as near as my eyes.
I find in the laughter of Christmas
        your voice,
and too many good-byes.

... and the Child was born that night
... and the Coming was blessed
... and the Star was the signal:

this Child is born
for Loving and for Dying

... and the Death was brief
... and the Love is always

Season's Greeting

Leave your life open
to the memories
and to the promises
of Christmas.

Christmas

In this season of love

when we know

more than ever

that we have forgotten nothing –

in this season of love

let us also give thanks

for

knowing

love.

Time turns
and at your doorstep waits
another Christmas
and another year...

    Time sings
    a gentle song for you to hear:
    "Let there be Christmas now,
    invite the coming year,
    what you have loved
    is always near."

Iowa Christmas Card

The days have turned to winter one more time,
the light behind your trees is pale with snow
that glow of giving gifts and singing songs
soon comes to warm the season and the heart.

And I try sending Christmas thoughts your way
to fill your house with comfort and with peace.
But most of all I hope and wish that you
will not be hurt too deeply, nor too long.

Hear the Children

We whose children died before us,
Do we share a greater wisdom?
True, beyond all earthly symbols?
Do we heed the heart's instruction?
Do we hear the children's voices?

Christmas is but one reminder
Of the legacy they left us.
Our dead, remembered children
Sing the same eternal song,
Send the same eternal message:

Peace is the question,
Love is the answer.

     David star or haunted cross,
     Crescent moon or sacred drum,
     Holy stream, ancestral shrine,
     Hymn or chant or temple dancer,
     All of us in Grieving Country,
     All of us share grievers' wisdom:

Peace is the question,
Love is the answer.

Listen

The new year will arrive again at midnight.
Your mind is heavy with remembering.
Your heart must ache before another chance
to quarrel with the emptiness of time.

Yes, New Year will walk in again at midnight.
And can you hear it speak of comfort, waiting,
of open doors and brighter rooms to enter,
of deeper meaning and of greater hope?

The new year will arrive and begs you:
        LISTEN.

Let There Be Light?

The New Year comes
when all the world is ready
for changes, resolutions —
great beginnings.

For us, to whom
that stroke of midnight means
a missing child remembered,
for us the new year comes
more like another darkness.

But let us not forget
that this may be the year
when love and hope and courage
find each other somewhere
in the darkness
            to lift their voice and speak:
            let there be light.

At New Year's, Time

Time does not touch
      the firmament of stars
with the simplicity
      of days and nights and years.
The rhythm of this smallness
      we call earth
is only whisper among galaxies.

Beyond the measured years
      which rise and fall,
beyond the calendars
      of human time and place,
the meaning of this smallness
      we call life
will find us somewhere
      in eternity.

New year, new year,
what will you bring?
how many smiles to smile,
how many songs to sing?

New year, new year,
what will you give?
how many children will
prosper and live?

New year, new year,
come and be kind.
let us have hope again
and peace of mind.

Endowment

Endowment

Hope gives us vision for regaining
the tenderness of memories.
Hope carries us through
to survival and healing.

Hope offers us courage
for acceptance and overcoming.
Hope gives us
new spirit and new laughter.

Hope is among the greatest gifts
to be found in time of sorrow.
But hope cannot restore
what is lost to death.
Hope can only go forward
and make us new.

Give space to hope in your life.

The children
who were with us
in the rush of life,
let them now be with us
in the peace of spirit.

Then and Now

They were my children, then.
Resounding voices, arguments and laughter –
Intense and wide awake at storytime –
In love with music, dance and birthday parties –

So serious about their great inventions –
So filled with promise, all-involved with life.

They are my children, now.
Remembered like a touching of the wind –
Remembered in the clarity of mornings –
Remembered in the smiles of other children –

Remembered like the charm of cradlesongs–
Alive in silence and in absence, present.
My children, now.

The children who died,
our children,
have left us a legacy
of consciousness and conscience.

The children who died
have taught us
the strength and worth
of knowing who we are,
taught us
the futility of pretensions,
taught us
the fallacy of prejudice.

The children who died,
our children,
have taught us
the tenderness found in sharing,
taught us
the loveliness of peace.

The children who died,
our children,
have left us a legacy
of vision and of light.

The past is part of us
and our future.
He who tells us to forget
does not understand
the past

      or

          the future.

Starting Small

Forgiveness is especially important
at times of grieving.

Forgiveness is especially important
for the griever.

Forgiveness must not be forced.

Begin with small easy things.
First forgive what
you can forgive without straining.
Then try forgiving some deeper
disappointments - one at a time.

Variations

Alone

    on winternights
    when darkness stands
    within your house,
    a sullen guest.

Alone

    at summernoon
    when beauty seems
    to be an empty space
    between the thing you see
    and what you feel...

Alone

    when some old song
    reverses time and place
    and you remember
    something that was best.
    And you are suddenly
    alive with love –
    and nothing else,
    not even sorrow
    breaks the glow

Alone?

You Live with Us

You live with us.
Your golden spirit lingers
in all the many tasks
        of our days.

The softness of your laughter
        calms this house,
when our minds are lost
        in grief or anger.
Your warmth returns with
        every memory
– a gift of love and care
        to help us live.
Your legacy of gentle wisdom gives us
the strength for going on
        without you, Randy.

You shine beyond the dark,
        a constant light.
And you will always be with
        mother, father, sister,
– in the simplicities of everyday
and in the grandeur of a thousand sunsets.
        You live with us.

Dedicated to the memory of Randy Misita.

Life has touched us
with the aching edge
of special grief.

Now
life is waiting
for the moment when
we can be comforted
by new compassion
and by deeper strength.

Then
life will touch us
with the timeless light
of special love.

Dedicated to Carol James.

Perennials

Good memories
are the perennials
that bloom again
after the hard winter of grief –
begins to yield to hope.

Epilogue

Beyond the history of grand events,
behind the memory of battles fought,
of freedoms lost and won,
there stand the silent legends of this earth,
the monuments of human joy and sorrow:
a sky of laughter on a sea of tears.

And they who cried the tears,
their children fallen,
sisters, brothers dead –
with lives washed over by relentless grief
they fought the battles seldom writ in stone.

And they who cried the tears
and laughed the laughter –
(though we may not be told
their name and place),
they share with us the history of coping,
of courage tested and enduring hope.

And they who cried the tears
and laughed the laughter
are history, as much as swords at war,
as much as grand events and freedoms won.

And all who ever mourned
– the whole world over –
are quietly with you and me today
to walk with us
through grief to hope and healing.

Written for the 13th Annual Conference of
The Compassionate Friends, July 6 – 8, 1990.

When Grieving Friends Meet

We are here together
in the radiance of our memories
and in the darkness of our loss.

The memories of days gone by
can be like northern lights,
outshining distance and night,
rising in wonder.

And sometimes
the radiance of our memories overcomes
the darkness of our loss.

We are here together
In the radiance of our memories
And in the service of our love.

Dedicated to the International TCF Conference, 2000 A.D.
Northern Lights of Healing
(Les Amis Compatissants du Canada).

Promise

Grief walks with you today,

your constant companion.

But in the morning, tomorrow,

the sunrise of hope waits for you.

Reminder

We who were left behind
to know the shadows –
We who were left behind
to touch the night –
We who were left behind
to heal the darkness
and to share this day –

We who have turned once more
to hope and loving,
though we were given graves
and lifeless children:
We hear them now,
these children and their song
reminding us,
reminding us again,
that we must fill the time
we spend in life
with understanding,
tenderness and peace.

Smiles

The smiles of our children fill this room
With memories of other summer days
When we could hear their laughter in the morning
When they could share the songs we sang at night.

The smiles of our children find us here
With all the loving that we gave them once
To bring us courage for another morning
To comfort us when we feel hurt at night.

The smiles of our children touch us now
With quiet hands of comfort and of hope.
Let them remind us as we meet today
That we are friends in our children's names.

Let us remember as we meet today
What our children taught us with their lives:
That love is never lost and love is never in vain.

Written for the Second National
Conference of In Loving Memory, 1997.

In Loving Memory

In spirit alike and with homage enduring, we came
Honoring love and remembrance in our child's name

Closely together in tender communion we stand
Holding each other's heart in a tremulous hand.
Children surround us that nobody's eye can see,
Children whose blessings bring solace to you and me.

Starting alone in the memory of heartbreaking fears,
Let us now share our sorrow and ease our tears.

In loving devotion let hope and fine courage arise,
Bestowed in the spirit of children beyond our eyes.
Until, in spite of the hurt from unbearable loss, we find
The treasure of friendship here and new peace of mind.

Written for the Fourth National Conference of
In Loving Memory, May 1999.

Paradox

The aching disappointments
of this life
seem smaller now –
they do not break me down
as they once did,
when I was not
so intimate with losing.

and yet –
each pain that touched me
bitterly, before
(and every hurt
and mourning done)
now casts its shadow darkly
to my eyes
whenever courage fades
and I must grieve again
the children who have died
a thousand years ago –
but yesterday.

Let us all
find love together,
let us sing
a loving song:
how this world
is bright with promise
how this world
can shine in peace
how this world
may last forever...

Let us all
find love together,
let us sing
a loving song:
how this world
will last forever,
if the children know
where they belong.

Journey

The journey from grief to hope

does not happen swiftly.

But it happens.

if you will let your heart

ride along.

Once, when you left us
in the gold of autumn,
we thought that you
were gone from us forever,
that you were lost to us
and we would never heal.
Yet we are close today,
more than we were before.
And now, because of you,
we see to other worlds,
we live in deeper regions.
You have become the bridge
from our commonplace
to great horizons,
the bridge from us
and our earthly time
to the abundance
of infinities.

Dedicated to Donald Trimmer.

Angel

Hope is the melancholy angel of grievers,
elusive and beautiful.
Hope is the light from nowhere,
telling us that we must reach
for the unknown promise
that waits to be fulfilled,
in a future we do not yet understand.

There are so many ways
to be alone –
    On winternights
    when darkness stands
    a sullen enemy
    inside your house...

    At summernoon
    when beauty seems
    to be an empty space
    between the thing you see
    and what you feel...

There are so many ways
to be alone –
    When some old song
    reverses time and place
    and you remember
    something that was best...
    when you are suddenly
    alive with love
    and nothing else,
    not even sorrow,
    breaks the glow...

Find all the light you can
when you're alone.

Soundings

The world may wonder:
        are we bound by death,
        we who have lost the child
        whose breath we shared.

The world should know
        though we may cry at night,
        we are not strangers
        to the art of laughter.

And sometimes
        we reach deeper into life.
        Has death then left us
        with a finer ear
        for listening to the song
        of other children?

(From One Who Knows)

I promise you, my friend,
I promise you
that you will feel
the warmth of spring again
that you will touch
the hands of children
and the lips of lovers
and the tenderness of Christmas again.

But here and now, my friend,
I promise only
small consolation:
Some morning you will see
beauty in your sorrow,
comfort in the wealth of love
remembered,
courage in the aching tide of days.

I promise you, my friend, I promise you
that you will understand
some day
some day
this pain which taught you
what depth and height
and greatness and devotion
one life can hold.
YOUR life, my friend.

The gift you give,

the love you feel,

the memory you cherish –

    These are the things

    by which your life

    endures and shines

Things You May Need to Say

It may take a while
before you can talk to those
who profess to love you
about the heartache
of broken promises,
absences or empty phrases.

Those friends who are important to you
need to hear how it hurts
to feel abandoned, or to be left behind
with broken promises, even small ones.

Whatever grief comes after yours
in this world,
it will benefit from your frankness.

Whether you are able to do it with caring,
or if you must do it with bluntness,
tell the world around you
that empty words, broken promises,
or absent friends
can be a griever's deepest disappointment.

Wish

I wish you gentle days
and quiet nights.
I wish you memories
to keep you strong.

I wish you time to smile
and time for song.

And then I wish you friends
to give you love,
when you are hurt and lost
and life is blind.

I wish you friends and love
and peace of mind.

Promise

In the rush of this life,
sadness does not always
have time enough.
So, if life insists
on a change of mood,
try giving in – gently.

Say "I miss you."
Say "I love you."

Say "So long."
And promise yourself
another sadness.
Tomorrow?

Index of Titles

Many of Sascha's poems are untitled. Those will be found in the Index of First Lines.

Index of First Lines

The Compassionate Friends

The Compassionate Friends (TCF) was begun in England in 1969 and has grown to become an international self-help organization offering friendship, understanding, and hope to families that have experienced the death of a child of any age, from any cause, including pregnancy loss. TCF is a nonprofit organization with no religious affiliation and no individual dues or fees.

In the United States and Puerto Rico, over 600 local TCF chapters reach out to bereaved parents and their families through regular self-help support group meetings, monthly newsletters, lending libraries of grief-related material, and memorial programs. Speakers are offered in the community to help others understand how to be supportive to bereaved friends and family members.

Together, these local chapters reach over 100,000 bereaved families on a regular basis. With the guidance of those who are further along in their grief, those more recently bereaved gradually find a "new normal" and begin to rebuild their lives. Some maintain their involvement with TCF, making the natural transition from being supported to becoming a helping hand reaching out to those who are just beginning their grief journey.

Bereaved families living where there is no local chapter can nevertheless receive ongoing support from The Compassionate Friends through TCF's website, which provides a multifaceted online support community led by trained volunteers. The site also is an excellent source of material and information about grief following the death of a child, sibling, or grandchild.

TCF's national office receives tens of thousands of inquiries annually from bereaved parents, siblings and grandparents, as well as from grief counselors and other professionals. Although the number grows each year, every one is answered with thoughtful, individual attention, just as they have been from the beginning.

> The Compassionate Friends
> 900 Jorie Boulevard, Ste. 78
> Oak Brook, Illinois 60523
> Toll free (877) 969-0010
> www.compassionatefriends.org